Susan B. Anthony & Elizabeth Cady Stanton

Early Suffragists

Harriet Isecke

Consultant

Marcus McArthur, Ph.D.
Department of History
Saint Louis University

Publishing Credits

Dona Herweck Rice, *Editor-in-Chief*
Lee Aucoin, *Creative Director*
Chris McIntyre, M.A.Ed., *Editorial Director*
Torrey Maloof, *Associate Editor*
Neri Garcia, *Senior Designer*
Stephanie Reid, *Photo Researcher*
Rachelle Cracchiolo, M.A.Ed., *Publisher*

Image Credits

Teacher Created Materials

5301 Oceanus Drive
Huntington Beach, CA 92649-1030
http://www.tcmpub.com

ISBN 978-1-4333-1506-0
© 2012 by Teacher Created Materials, Inc.

Table of Contents

We Want Equal Rights, Too!

When the United States became a country, women had very few rights. Women could not own **property** or go to most colleges. Women were not allowed to vote.

Many brave women fought to get equal rights. They gave speeches. They marched. Their work was dangerous. Some women were hurt. Some were thrown in jail. But, this did not stop them. The fight for the women's vote was called the **Suffrage** (SUHF-rij) Movement.

Elizabeth Cady Stanton and Susan B. Anthony were two leaders of the Suffrage Movement. They were called **suffragists**. Suffragists support the idea of giving the right to vote to other people, especially women. Cady Stanton and Anthony were close friends. They made a great team. Anthony organized everything. She ran things well. Cady Stanton liked to write and give speeches.

Susan B. Anthony (left) and Elizabeth Cady Stanton (right)

Cady Stanton and Anthony had many goals, but their main goal was getting women the right to vote.

Not For Me!

Susan B. Anthony decided she did not want to get married. She valued her freedom and did not want to lose her independence. She also wanted as much time as possible to focus on women's rights.

An Equal Marriage

Cady Stanton did decide to marry. But, her husband believed in equal rights for women, too. In their ceremony the couple did not include the word *obey*. They wanted their marriage to be equal. Cady Stanton also kept her last name. She was not referred to as Mrs. Henry Stanton, but rather Elizabeth Cady Stanton.

Some people were afraid to let women vote. There were those who thought it would hurt the country. They thought it would hurt families. Others thought women were not smart enough to vote. They thought women should stay at home. But, women like Anthony and Cady Stanton did not give up. They kept fighting!

Meet the Leaders

Elizabeth Cady Stanton

Elizabeth Cady Stanton was born on November 12, 1815, in New York. Her father was a lawyer and a judge. Her mother came from a wealthy family. The Cady family was big! The Cadys had 11 children. But, five of them died when they were babies. When Cady Stanton was 11 years old, her only remaining brother died. He was just 20 years old.

Cady Stanton with one of her children

Cady Stanton was sad when her brother died. Her father was heartbroken. He could not believe he had lost all his sons. He told Cady Stanton that he wished she were a boy. From that moment on, Cady Stanton was determined to be just as brave and courageous as boys. She wanted to prove to her father that girls could do everything that boys could do.

Cady Stanton loved to read and write. Because her father was a lawyer, and later a judge, she had access to lots of law books. That is how she began to learn about the laws in the United States. She soon learned how unfair these laws were to women and wanted to change them.

An Important Influence

Cady Stanton's cousin, Gerrit Smith, was an **abolitionist** (ab-uh-LISH-uh-nist). He was an important leader in the movement to end slavery. Smith also believed in equal rights for women. Cady Stanton loved visiting Smith at his house. He always had large groups of abolitionists and **activists** there. These people wanted to change laws in the country. Cady Stanton loved to hear their ideas and have discussions with them.

Cady Stanton wanted to end slavery and attended many abolitionist meetings like this one.

Gerrit Smith

Call Me Henry

Cady Stanton met her husband, Henry Stanton, at one of Smith's parties. After their marriage, Cady Stanton would call her husband Henry. This may not seem strange, since that was his name. However, she called him Henry in front of strangers. A women was not supposed to refer to her husband by his first name in polite society. This behavior shocked a lot of people. But, Cady Stanton did not let people's reactions bother her. She continued to call him Henry.

Henry Brewster Stanton

Susan B. Anthony

Susan B. Anthony

Susan B. Anthony was born on February 15, 1820, in Massachusetts. Anthony grew up in a **Quaker** (KWEY-ker) family. Quakers led simple lives. They did not believe in singing and dancing. They wore plain clothing. Quakers believed in equality. They were against slavery and thought that both men and women should be treated the same.

Quaker children, both boys and girls, attended school. It was unusual at this time for girls to go to school. Anthony not only went to school, she later became a teacher. She taught for ten years. When Anthony asked to be paid the same amount of money as male teachers, she was told no. Anthony quit teaching and instead focused on social problems, such as women's rights and ending slavery.

Anthony wanted to help women get equal rights. She also wanted to help end slavery. She started giving speeches and writing **petitions**. The petitions asked that laws in the United States be changed. If a lot of people signed the petitions, then maybe the United States government would change the laws. Anthony was determined to make a difference.

Anthony's childhood home in Massachusetts

Anthony's Active Family

Anthony's parents worked to stop slavery. They were abolitionists. They also worked for the **Temperance** Movement. This movement wanted to reduce, or limit, the sale of alcohol. Anthony's parents also wanted their daughters to go to the local school. When the local school would not let his girls attend, Anthony's father opened a school in their home.

Daughters of Temperance

Anthony found out that women were not allowed in the local temperance group. So, she joined the Daughters of Temperance. This was an all-women's group. The group tried to help women whose husbands drank too much alcohol. When the men drank too much, they did not think clearly. Some of them did not feed their families. Others were violent.

This man is signing a temperance pledge, in which he promises to give up drinking alcohol.

A Promise Is Made

At the antislavery meeting in London, Cady Stanton met Lucretia (loo-KREE-shuh) Mott. Mott was a famous abolitionist. She also supported women's rights. The two women made a promise to each other. They were going to hold the first ever meeting on women's rights. They held the Woman's Rights Convention in 1848 in Seneca Falls, New York.

The Women's Declaration

At the Woman's Rights Convention, Cady Stanton read the *Declaration of Sentiments*. She used the Declaration of Independence as a model. But, in her declaration she wrote that both "men and women are created equal." Many of the women at the convention signed this declaration.

A Friendship Begins
Cady Stanton and Anthony Meet

In 1840, Cady Stanton traveled to London. She went to an antislavery meeting with her husband. The men running the meeting told the women to sit in the back of the room. They said the women could not speak. They could only listen. This upset Cady Stanton. She wanted a change.

Lucretia Mott

Cady Stanton's *Declaration of Sentiments*

DECLARATION OF SENTIMENTS.

When, in the course of human events, it becomes necessary for one portion of the family of man to assume among the people of the earth a position different from that which they have hitherto occupied, but one to which the laws of nature and of nature's God entitle them, a decent respect to the opinions of mankind requires that they should declare the causes that impel them to such a course.

We hold these truths to be self-evident: that all men and women are created equal; that they are endowed by their Creator with certain inalienable rights, that among these are life, liberty, and the pursuit of happiness; that to secure these rights governments are instituted, deriving their just powers from the consent of the governed. Whenever any form of government becomes destructive of these ends, it is the right of those who suffer from it to refuse allegiance to it, and to insist upon the institution of a new government, laying its foundation on such principles, and organizing its powers in such form as to them shall seem most likely to effect their safety and happiness. Prudence, indeed, will dictate that governments long established should not be changed for light and transient causes; and accordingly, all experience hath shown that mankind are more disposed to suffer, while evils are sufferable, than to right themselves by abolishing the forms to which they were accustomed. But when a long train of abuses and usurpations, pursuing invariably the same object evinces a design to reduce them under absolute despotism, it is their duty to throw off such government, and to provide new guards for their future security. Such has been the patient sufferance of the women under this government, and such is now the necessity which constrains them to demand the equal station to which they are entitled.

The history of mankind is a history of repeated injuries and usurpations on the part of man toward woman, having in direct object the establishment of an absolute tyranny over her. To prove this, let facts be submitted to a candid world.

Cady Stanton addressing the first Woman's Rights
Convention in 1848, in Seneca Falls, New York

In 1848, Cady Stanton helped organize an important meeting in Seneca Falls, New York. It was the first Woman's Rights **Convention**. At the convention, Cady Stanton gave a key speech. She made three main points. She said women are equal to men. Women must have the same rights as men. And, women must be allowed to vote. These were bold things to say during this time.

Three years later, Cady Stanton met Anthony. Anthony was tired of working in activist groups run by men. She was impressed with Cady Stanton's knowledge and writing skills. And, she had heard what Cady Stanton did at Seneca Falls. The two women decided to work together. They began planning ways to help women.

Cady Stanton taught Anthony about the law. Sometimes Cady Stanton would get very busy taking care of her seven children. So, Anthony would step in and help. She would organize meetings and give speeches. The two women made a great team.

Changing a Bad Law

At one time, married women in the United States could not own property. They could not buy land or own a house. They were also not allowed to keep the **wages** (WEYJ-ez) they earned from their jobs. And, they did not have **custody** or legal rights for their children. Anthony and Cady Stanton knew a change needed to be made. So, the two women focused their attention on changing the property laws in New York.

Anthony was not married and did not have children. This left her with more time to organize the fight. She traveled around the state of New York. She spoke in 54 counties! Cady Stanton did the research and wrote the speeches.

In 1860, Cady Stanton gave a powerful speech in front of New York's lawmakers. She told them why women needed to have rights. The speech worked! A new law was passed. Married women could now own property.

Some men were not happy with the progress suffragists were making. They started forming antisuffrage groups.

The steps, from bottom to top:

SLAVERY
HOUSE DRUDGERY
SHOP WORK
CLERKS · AGENTS · MAIDS
TEACHERS · CARETAKERS
BOOKKEEPING · STENOGRAPHY
NURSE · GOVERNESS
PRIVATE SECRETARY
ARTS · CRAFTS · SCIENCE
BUSINESS AFFAIRS
SCHOOL AFFAIRS
CHURCH & CHARITIES
WAR WORKERS
PUBLIC OFFICE
GOVERNMENT OFFICE
LAW · MEDICINE
EQUAL SUFFRAGE
NOTARY PUBLIC
WAGE EQUALITY
POLITICAL APPOINTMENTS
POSITIONS OF TRUST
HIGH ELECTIVE OFFICES
EXECUTIVE
LEGISLATIVE
CONGRESS
GOVERNORSHIP
SENATE
PRESIDENCY

This political cartoon shows all the steps women had to climb before reaching equal suffrage.

Please Sign Here

Anthony worked hard to collect signatures from those who supported women's rights. By 1854, she had over 10,000 signatures on her petition. Anthony's petition asked for voting and property rights for women. She presented her petition to New York lawmakers.

New Rights

New laws passed in 1860 gave women in New York new rights. A married woman living in the state of New York could now run a business. She could also control her own money.

13

Men Only

The Fourteenth Amendment to the United States Constitution gave African American men rights, but it did not help women. Cady Stanton was upset that the word *male* was included in this amendment. She was worried that African American men would soon get the right to vote, and women would remain left out of the United States Constitution.

Universal Suffrage

Cady Stanton and Anthony, along with other suffragists, wanted to get a petition to the House of Representatives. The petition was for universal suffrage. That means that they wanted everyone to have the right to vote. Congressman Thaddeus Stevens gave the petition to the House of Representatives in 1866.

A petition for universal suffrage signed by Cady Stanton and Anthony

Forming Groups
Fighting for Equal Rights

In 1866, the National Woman's Rights Convention had a meeting. Both Cady Stanton and Anthony spoke at the meeting. They wanted to start a group that would give the same rights to everyone in the United States. This group would fight for the rights of African Americans and women. The group was called the American Equal Rights **Association** (AERA).

A PETITION FOR UNIVERSAL SUFFRAGE.

To the Senate and House of Representatives:

The undersigned, Women of the United States, respectfully ask an amendment of the Constitution that shall prohibit the several States from disfranchising any of their citizens on the ground of sex.

In making our demand for Suffrage, we would call your attention to the fact that we represent fifteen million people—one half the entire population of the country—intelligent, virtuous, native-born American citizens; and yet stand outside the pale of political recognition.

The Constitution classes us as "free people," and counts us whole persons in the basis of representation; and yet are we governed without our consent, compelled to pay taxes without appeal, and punished for violations of law without choice of judge or juror.

The experience of all ages, the Declarations of the Fathers, the Statute Laws of our own day, and the fearful revolution through which we have just passed, all prove the uncertain tenure of life, liberty and property so long as the ballot—the only weapon of self-protection—is not in the hand of every citizen.

Therefore, as you are now amending the Constitution, and, in harmony with advancing civilization, placing new safeguards round the individual rights of four millions of emancipated slaves, we ask that you extend the right of Suffrage to Woman—the only remaining class of disfranchised citizens—and thus fulfil your Constitutional obligation "to Guarantee to every State in the Union a Republican form of Government."

As all partial application of Republican principles must ever breed a complicated legislation as well as a discontented people, we would pray your Honorable Body, in order to simplify the machinery of government and ensure domestic tranquility, that you legislate hereafter for persons, citizens, tax-payers, and not for class or caste.

For justice and equality your petitioners will ever pray.

NAMES.	RESIDENCE.
Elizabeth Stanton	New York
Susan B. Anthony	Rochester—N.Y.
Antoinette Brown Blackwell	No York
Lucy Stone	Newark N. Jersey
Joanna S. Morse	48 Livingston, Brooklyn
Ernestine L. Rose	New York
Harriet E. Eaton	6. West 14 Street N.Y
Catharine C. Wilkeson	83 Clinton Place

Flyer for the 11th National Woman's Rights Conference in 1866

When the AERA formed, the Civil War had ended. Slaves had been freed in the South. People asked for a change to the United States Constitution. In 1868, the Fourteenth **Amendment** (uh-MEND-muhnt) was passed. This amendment said that all states had to give rights to African American men. Anthony and Cady Stanton said that this amendment should give rights to women, as well. Some of the women in the AERA did not agree. They said that African American men should have rights first.

Anthony and Cady Stanton were upset. They asked the AERA for help with the Fifteenth Amendment. This amendment would give African American men the right to vote. Anthony and Cady Stanton wanted to make sure women were included in this one.

The Group Splits

Some members of AERA agreed with Anthony and Cady Stanton and wanted women to be included in the Fifteenth Amendment. They said all United States **citizens** (SIT-uh-zuhnz) should be able to vote. Other members did not agree. They were worried that if women were included in the amendment it would not pass. The group fought and fought. They could not agree. So, they split into two groups.

Anthony and Cady Stanton's new group was called the National Woman Suffrage Association (NWSA). The other group was called the American Woman Suffrage Association (AWSA). It was a sad time for women. It was not good for them to work separately.

Anthony and Cady Stanton wanted more people to hear what they thought. So in 1868, they started a newspaper. It was called *The Revolution*. Anthony ran the paper. Cady Stanton was the main writer. The paper gave them a chance to have people read their ideas. They were able to show others the importance of women's rights.

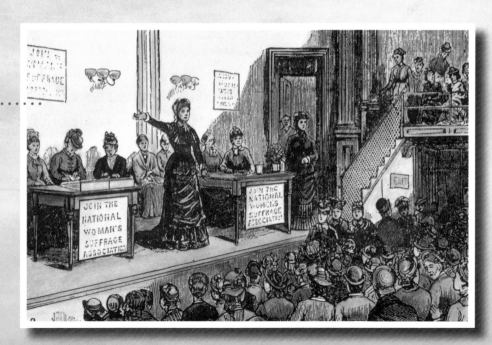

Cady Stanton and Anthony spoke at a National Woman Suffrage Association (NWSA) meeting.

The first issue of *The Revolution* was published in 1868.

The Fifteenth Amendment

A Newspaper for Women's Rights

The Revolution was a weekly women's rights newspaper. The paper did not make the women any money. In fact, Anthony had to use $10,000 of her own money to pay off the debt created by the newspaper. Anthony earned that money by giving speeches. She did not mind that the newspaper was not making money. She was happy that women's voices were being heard. However, in 1872, Anthony had to stop publishing the newspaper. She could not afford to pay the bills anymore.

No Votes for Women

In 1870, the Fifteenth Amendment was added to the United States Constitution. It said a citizen could vote regardless of race or color. However, just like Cady Stanton and Anthony had feared, women were not included in the amendment.

It Is Time to Vote!

Anthony Breaks the Law

Anthony and other women were tired of waiting. They had fought to change the law so that women could vote, but they had been unsuccessful. Anthony decided it was time to break the law.

On November 1, 1872, Anthony walked up to the men at the voting booth. She asked for a ballot. The men said that they could not let her vote. They said the constitution of the state of New York only allowed men to vote. Anthony argued that the Fourteenth Amendment to the United States Constitution said that she was a citizen. And if she was a citizen, she should be allowed to vote. The men saw that there was no way to win the argument. So, they let her vote.

Two weeks later, Anthony was arrested. She was put on trial. The **jury** only had men. Women were not allowed to be **jurors** at that time in New York. The judge told the men to find Anthony guilty. Anthony was angry and spoke her mind in front of the court.

This cartoon of Anthony was drawn in 1873, at the time of her trial.

This suffragist cartoon shows that even men who were not good citizens could vote. But, women could be nurses or doctors and still could not vote.

But Article I Says...
The first **article** in the Fourteenth Amendment says that any native-born or **naturalized** person is a citizen of the United States. Anthony claimed that this amendment said she was a citizen of the United States and, therefore, she had the right to vote.

Anthony Speaks Up
When the judge asked if Anthony had anything to say, she replied, "I have many things to say!" She said the only chance for women to have **justice** was for them to break the law as she had done. The judge tried to stop Anthony during her speech, but she just kept talking. She wanted to make sure her voice was heard.

AN
ACCOUNT OF THE PROCEEDINGS
ON THE
TRIAL OF
SUSAN B. ANTHONY,
ON THE
Charge of Illegal Voting,
AT THE
PRESIDENTIAL ELECTION IN NOV., 1872,
AND ON THE
TRIAL OF
BEVERLY W. JONES, EDWIN T. MARSH
AND WILLIAM B. HALL,
THE INSPECTORS OF ELECTION BY WHOM HER VOTE WAS RECEIVED.

ROCHESTER. N.Y.:
DAILY DEMOCRAT AND CHRONICLE BOOK PRINT, 2 WEST MAIN ST.

The trial of Susan B. Anthony was a big news story at the time.

A Matter of Safety

In the winter of 1875, Anthony gave a speech she titled "Social **Purity**." She gave it at the Grand Opera House in Chicago. There was a very large crowd, and they were excited to hear what she had to say.

Anthony gave a strong speech. She said that women did not drink as much alcohol as men. But, women suffered more because of it. She said that women had to depend on men for food. They had to depend on men for shelter. If husbands spent all their time and money drinking, their wives and children were the ones that suffered. She argued that women would not be safe until they had equal rights.

The people who sold alcohol did not like this. They thought if women could vote, it would be bad for business. They thought women would vote to stop the sale of all alcohol! This would mean that they would lose their jobs. So, they fought hard against women's suffrage.

This cartoon shows women waging war on alcohol.

Carry Nation, a temperance leader, was known for attacking bars with her ax.

Stop the Women's Vote

A **lobby** is a group of people who try to get laws made that will help them. The Liquor (LIK-er) Lobby worked against women's suffrage. Groups formed against the Liquor Lobby. These were called temperance groups.

Forcing the Nation

Anthony said that sometimes the United States had to be forced to give rights to people. The United States had been forced to stop slavery and to let free African American men vote. Now they needed to be forced to give women rights.

Women in the Temperance Movement wanted to make selling, buying, and drinking alcohol against the law. They felt it was hurting their families.

Thinking Globally

By 1882, Cady Stanton's children were old enough that she could start traveling again. She decided to go to Europe, since two of her older children were living there at the time. She wanted to see them. But, that was not the only reason she went.

Things were bad for women all over the world at this time, and Cady Stanton wanted to start a new group. She wanted it to be **international** (in-ter-NASH-uh-null). She thought women from all over the world should work together to improve their lives. Anthony went to Europe to join Cady Stanton, and there they planned a huge meeting.

The International Council of Women (ICW) met in 1888, in Washington, DC. It was the biggest meeting of its time. Women came from many different places. Their goal was to form a group of women in each country around the world. The groups would then work together and help each other. The United States formed its group right away. But, the other countries did not. Cady Stanton and Anthony felt let down. Things did not work out the way they had hoped.

Leaders of the ICW, including Anthony (second from left, front row) and Cady Stanton (third from right, front row)

A flyer for the International Council of Women (ICW) conference

A Special Day

The first meeting of the International Council of Women was to take place on a special day. That day was the 40th anniversary of the first Woman's Rights Convention in Seneca Falls, New York. This was the meeting that Cady Stanton and Mott had planned when they met in England for the first time.

Women's History Is Written

In the 1880s, Cady Stanton and Anthony worked on another big project. They published the *History of Woman Suffrage*. It was in three large **volumes**. Cady Stanton's daughter, Harriot, helped them write it. Later, Anthony added three more volumes to the collection.

Reunited in 1890

The Suffrage Movement was still split into two groups. Cady Stanton and Anthony's group was the National Woman Suffrage Association (NWSA). It fought against the Fifteenth Amendment. They were mad that the amendment did not include women.

The NWSA had big goals. Anthony thought working on women's right to vote was most important. But, Cady Stanton wanted to change other things, too. She thought women should be able to get the jobs they wanted. She thought they should be able to get **divorces** if they needed them. She thought that women's dress **codes** were too strict.

While Cady Stanton and Anthony were working hard with their group, the American Woman Suffrage Association (AWSA) was working hard, too. However, both groups realized they would be stronger working together. Since the Fifteenth Amendment had already passed by this time, the groups were able to put their differences aside and join forces again.

The National American Woman Suffrage Association (NAWSA) in 1919

> "WOMEN ARE CITIZENS OF THE UNITED STATES, ENTITLED TO ALL THE RIGHTS, PRIVILEGES AND IMMUNITIES GUARANTEED TO CITIZENS BY THE NATIONAL GOVERNMENT."

NATIONAL American WOMAN SUFFRAGE ASSOCIATION
OF THE UNITED STATES.

Miss Anne Fitzhugh Miller having paid Fifty Dollars is a LIFE MEMBER of this Association, entitled to the rights and privileges thereof.

No. 53.

Elizabeth Cady Stanton
Honorary President.

Susan B. Anthony
President.

Harriet Taylor Upton
Treasurer.

HINGTON, D. C., February 15, 1900.

This is a National American Woman Suffrage Association membership card signed by Cady Stanton and Anthony.

The new group was called the National American Woman Suffrage Association (NAWSA). The NAWSA became the biggest suffrage group in the United States. Cady Stanton was selected to be the president of the new group.

A Dream Comes True

At this time, there were some changes that made women's lives better. Harriot Stanton was able to do something that her mother, Elizabeth Cady Stanton, only dreamed of doing. She graduated from Vassar College with a degree in mathematics.

The Big Group

Although Anthony was now the more popular suffragist, Cady Stanton was selected to be president of the group. Anthony had asked the women to vote for Cady Stanton. Anthony did not feel comfortable being president when Cady Stanton was the reason she was a member of the Suffrage Movement in the first place.

Punishing Cady Stanton

Cady Stanton was the first president of the NAWSA. But, in 1892 she was forced out of the group for writing *The Woman's Bible*. Anthony asked the NAWSA not to punish Stanton for writing it, but the women voted 53 to 41 in favor of parting ways with Cady Stanton. Cady Stanton was angry that she was no longer a member of the group that she had started.

President Anthony

The NAWSA's new president was now Anthony. Cady Stanton asked Anthony to resign, or leave the group. She thought Anthony should support her and not the NAWSA's decision. Anthony did not know what to do. She disagreed with the NAWSA's actions and wanted to support her friend. But in the end, Anthony decided to remain with the NAWSA and serve as its president.

Big Controversy

A **controversy** is when people strongly disagree on something. Cady Stanton created a big controversy in 1895.

Cady Stanton read the Bible. She thought that some of the women in it were strong. But she also thought that some parts of the Bible did not respect women. Many people based their treatment of women on the words of the Bible. Cady Stanton thought the words should be rewritten to help change the treatment of women. She decided to rewrite the Bible.

This idea was very **controversial** (kon-truh-VUR-shuhl). Even some women in the NAWSA did not support it. Changing the Bible went against the beliefs of many people. But changing people's beliefs about women was exactly what Cady Stanton wanted to do.

Cady Stanton began writing *The Woman's Bible* in 1892. It was published in 1895. There were things in the book that shocked people. The new bible did not specifically say that God is a woman, but it did hint at that idea.

Anthony (standing)
and Cady Stanton

Cady Stanton's notes for
The Woman's Bible

Failure Is Impossible

Cady Stanton spent her final years with her children and grandchildren. She continued to write about women's rights for newspapers, as well. She told people what she thought and people listened. In 1902, Cady Stanton died just two weeks before her 87th birthday. Anthony thought her heart would break. She told a reporter, "I'm too crushed to speak."

By then, Anthony was sick, too. Her doctor told her to stop working. But, Anthony did not want to stop. She thought there was still too much important work to be done.

In 1906, Anthony was 86 years old. She spoke at a NAWSA meeting. She said that women would get to vote soon and that "Failure is impossible!" A few weeks later, Anthony died.

Cady Stanton and Anthony did not live to see women get the right to vote. But, their hard work made a difference. They **paved** the way and set the example for future women suffragists. It was because of their bravery that women were finally given the right to vote in 1920. Anthony and Cady Stanton will always be remembered as successful **reformers** for the women's rights movement.

A suffragist holds a banner in 1915 with Anthony's famous phrase on it.

Cady Stanton's death as reported in a newspaper

State by State

Some states allowed women to vote before other states. In 1890, Wyoming became the first state to allow women to vote. Ten years later, Utah, Colorado, and Idaho also allowed women to vote.

Finally!

The Nineteenth Amendment gave women the right to vote. The Senate first voted on the Nineteenth Amendment in October 1918. It failed by three votes. The Senate finally passed the amendment in 1919. But, it did not become law until 1920.

The Nineteenth Amendment

Glossary

abolitionist—a person who fights against slavery

activists—people who take action to change society

amendment—an official change to the United States Constitution

article—a separate part of a document that deals with a single subject

association—an organization of people with a common purpose

citizens—people who are members of a state or government and are protected by it

codes—a collection of laws or rules

controversial—an idea or subject about which people have different and strong opinions

controversy—something about which there is a great difference of opinion

convention—a formal gathering of members

custody—to have legal control of a child

divorces—marriages that have legally ended

international—involving more than one country or nation

jurors—members of a jury

jury—a group of people who decide whether a person on trial for a crime is guilty or innocent

justice—the act of being treated fairly or justly

lobby—a group of people who try to get laws made that will help them

naturalized—to be born a citizen, or to be given the rights of citizenship

paved—to have prepared a smooth, easy way

petitions—requests to change something

property—something that is owned like lands, goods, or money

purity—the state of being pure or free from guilt or evil; innocence

Quaker—a member of the religious group called Society of Friends

reformers—people that make things better by removing faults

suffrage—the right to vote

suffragists—people who thought women should be allowed to vote

temperance—the use of little or no alcohol

volumes—a series of books that forms a collection or a complete work

wages—money earned for work

Index

Your Turn!

From the time the first settlers arrived in America, women were treated as second-class citizens. They were not allowed to go to school, work outside the home in most jobs, own property, or vote. To reach equality with men, they had to work toward major changes.

View from the Bottom

Study the political cartoon above. Read as many of the words on the ladder as possible. Then, imagine how the young woman in the carton must be feeling. Write a diary entry about equal rights from the point of view of the young woman.